MODERN ROSES

AN ILLUSTRATED GUIDE TO VARIETIES, CULTIVATION AND CARE, WITH
STEP-BY-STEP INSTRUCTIONS AND OVER 150 BEAUTIFUL PHOTOGRAPHS

Andrew Mikolajski

Consultant: Lin Hawthorne
Photography by Marie O'Hara

southwater

This edition is published by Southwater
an imprint of Anness Publishing Ltd
Blaby Road, Wigston, Leicestershire LE18 4SE
info@anness.com

www.southwaterbooks.com; www.annesspublishing.com

If you like the images in this book and would like to investigate
using them for publishing, promotions or advertising, please visit
our website www.practicalpictures.com for more information.

A CIP catalogue record for this book is available from the British Library.

Publisher: Joanna Lorenz
Senior Editor: Cathy Marriott
Designer: Michael Morey
Production Controller: Mai-Ling Collyer

PUBLISHER'S NOTE
Although the advice and information in this book are believed to be accurate and true at the time
of going to press, neither the authors nor the publisher can accept any legal responsibility or liability
for any errors or omissions that may have been made nor for any inaccuracies nor for any loss,
harm or injury that comes about from following instructions or advice in this book.

■ HALF TITLE PAGE
'Big Purple'

■ FRONTISPIECE
'Hakuun'

■ TITLE PAGE
'Lovers' Meeting'

■ LEFT
'Freedom'

■ OPPOSITE LEFT
'National Trust'

■ OPPOSITE RIGHT
'Blue Moon'

MODERN ROSES

Contents

Introduction

*T*he rose is the quintessential flower of summer. Most modern varieties combine a cast-iron constitution with an unrivalled length of flowering. Some are dainty and elegant, others richly coloured show-stoppers, and many are deliciously fragrant. Besides their value in beds and borders, some can be used for ground cover, while those with a neat, compact habit are ideal for growing in a container, either on the terrace or a patio. There are even modern roses that have been bred to provide long-lasting blooms for the flower arranger. This book shows you how to grow and care for all these essential plants, and illustrates some of the most outstanding modern roses now available.

■ RIGHT
Modern roses reward the gardener
with flowers all summer.

The history of the modern rose

The history of the modern rose is usually held to have begun in 1867 with the introduction of 'La France'. Raised by Jean Guillot in France, it was considered an important novelty in rose breeding because it combined the long season and elegant flower shape of Chinese tea roses, from which it was descended, with the robust habit and hardiness of European roses.

'La France' was initially classified as a hybrid perpetual, a group of roses now more or less obsolete because they are leggy and difficult to place in the garden. It was soon realized, however, that this was a new type of

■ LEFT
The radiant orange-red 'Top Marks' is a classic example of a dwarf cluster-flowered rose.

■ BELOW
One of the best yellow roses, 'Arthur Bell' shines out dramatically against a background of clipped yew.

rose, and the class hybrid tea was created. Today, hybrid teas are more correctly, if less elegantly, known as large-flowered bush roses.

Further selection and breeding refined the type, but the most significant breakthrough occurred early in the 20th century and involved the bright yellow *R. foetida* from central Asia (confusingly known as the Austrian briar). The species has two forms, 'Bicolor' (with vivid orange petals and a yellow reverse) and 'Persiana' (double flowers) that were also used, creating an unprecedented colour range

■ RIGHT
'White Pet', one of the first miniature
roses, has stood the test of time.

including exciting bicolour and
striped roses. The heyday of the old
roses, with their somewhat restricted
palette of white, pink and maroon,
was over.

The new hybrid teas were bred
with polyanthas — another largely
obsolete rose group, which yields
trusses of small flowers – to increase
the flower size of the latter. The
resulting roses were classified as
hybrid polyanthas. Further breeding,
notably in Britain, Denmark and the
USA, produced roses with even larger
flowers, though never as large as those
of the hybrid tea.

'Rochester', introduced in 1934,
was the first rose to be classified as
a floribunda – producing smallish
flowers in large sprays – but although
the term was widely used, it never
gained universal recognition. Other
classifications included "floribunda
hybrid-tea type" (for plants with large
flowers) and "grandiflora" (for very
tall roses), which meant that different
terms were being used simultaneously
for a range of roses that had certain
broad similarities. Nowadays, all such
roses are classified as cluster-flowered
bush roses.

These two groups (the hybrid tea
and floribunda) gradually came to
dominate the rose market, being both
easy to grow and reliable, and having
a long flowering season. They proved
ideal for bedding, and are still planted
en masse for a bold display of solid
blocks of colour in public parks and
gardens. Towards the end of the
20th century, however, they lost
some of their dominance with the
revival of interest in cottage gardens
in the style of the Edwardian garden
designer Gertrude Jekyll. Old roses
enjoyed a renaissance. Inevitably,
breeders began looking for novelties
to win back the attention of the
gardening fraternity, and further
hybridization produced several new
classes. There are now roses for all
manner of garden applications,
including so-called patio roses,
ground-cover roses, and miniatures.
The recent trend towards dwarf,
compact roses is remarkable.
Miniature varieties first appeared
early in the 19th century, but were
regarded as little more than novelties
for about 150 years. Today, with
ever smaller gardens, their appeal
has never been greater, and new
varieties regularly appear to tempt
the gardener (for further details
of modern rose groups, see
Classification and garden use).

Modern roses in the garden

Such is the diversity of modern roses that their use in the garden is virtually unlimited. Whether you are looking for plants large or small, with strong or muted colours, rich perfume, a long flowering season, or for growing in containers, there is a rose to answer every need.

Bedding

For many gardeners, the large- and cluster-flowered roses are synonymous with bedding. A uniform effect is best created by sticking to one variety. If you want to mix varieties, check the final heights

MODERN ROSES FOR BEDDING SCHEMES
'Alexander' (red)
'Allgold' (yellow)
'Chinatown' (golden-yellow)
'Elina' (ivory-white)
'Iceberg' (white)
'Just Joey' (orange)
'Sexy Rexy' (light rose-pink)
'Super Star' (vermilion)

and group the tallest at the back of the border (or in the centre of an island bed), with shorter-growing varieties in front. By planting miniatures at their feet, you can create a bed that is roughly triangular in cross-section.

For maximum impact, use the luminous 'Super Star', 'Precious Platinum' or 'Drummer Boy', which are among the best of the reds. 'Allgold' is a good yellow that keeps its colour well, while among the salmon-orange roses 'Anne Harkness' and 'Amber Queen' are outstanding. Possibly even more eye-catching are those that combine two colours, such as 'Piccadilly' (scarlet and yellow), 'Oranges and Lemons' (yellow, striped scarlet) and 'Circus' (whose flowers open yellow, mature to red,

■ RIGHT
Brilliant scarlet 'Fred Loads' sets alight
a planting of herbaceous perennials.

and fade to orange, buff and pink).
For more subtle schemes, 'Iceberg',
'Margaret Merril' and 'Pascali' are
some of the most rain-resistant
whites. It would be invidious to
choose among the pinks, since there
are so many excellent candidates, but
'Sexy Rexy' has a good clear colour,
while 'Queen Elizabeth', a deeper
cyclamen-pink, is one of the most
versatile of all roses.

You can edge your rose bed with
other bedding plants. Pelargoniums
have a long flowering season and
come in a similar colour range
(though there is no yellow).
Particularly useful are annuals such
as African and French marigolds
(*Tagetes*), which come in a cheery
yellow or orange and attract beneficial
insects that prey on aphids (see Pests,
diseases and other disorders). If you
wish to add a touch of blue, a colour
which roses cannot offer, use
ageratum or lobelia.

Standards

Standard roses are not trained as
such, but are normal bush roses
grafted on to stems of a vigorous
species such as *Rosa rugosa* (see
Propagation). They are available as
full standards on a stem about 1.2m

(4ft) high, or half-standards which
are about 75cm (2½ft) high. They
produce a lollipop shape, though
grafted ground-cover roses (see

■ ABOVE
For added scent in the garden, you could
try combining roses with annual tobacco
(*Nicotiana*) plants.

Ground-cover roses) and climbers
produce a weeping tree.

You can deploy standards in a
formal scheme to striking effect.
They can rise above a sea of bedding
roses, either to contrast with or
complement them, or they can be
used in a small garden to line a
path, creating a kind of miniature,
tree-lined avenue. Standards can also
be used individually as eye-catchers to
mark the end of a vista, or in a lawn,
or in pairs to mark the start of a
path or a flight of steps. To add style
to a doorway, plant standards in pots,
but when bare in winter they will
need to be replaced by evergreen
hollies (*Ilex*) or bays (*Laurus nobilis*).

■ LEFT
The cluster-flowered 'Eye Paint'
planted *en masse* beneath
Gleditschia triacanthos 'Sunburst'.

weeds. Unlike other ground-cover plants, they do not always form weed-suppressing mats, and weeding through the thorny stems can be a thankless task.

Other uses

Some modern roses can be planted as hedges. While they have an unrivalled flowering season among hedging plants, they do have the disadvantage of being deciduous, and cannot provide a year-round barrier. Two fine varieties are 'Chinatown' (golden-yellow) and 'Queen Elizabeth' (pink), both of which reach 2m (6½ft) or more if lightly pruned (see Pruning). Other roses will form lower hedges, rugosas being especially effective with their tough, attractive foliage. Miniatures, such as 'Baby Masquerade', make an attractive low hedge or border edging in place of the traditional box or lavender.

Some modern roses also make highly effective lawn specimens. 'Chinatown' is a very good candidate, but 'Iceberg' is better still. Requiring only the minimum of pruning over a number of years, it will develop into an impressive shrub whose shape lives up to its name.

Roses as ground cover

Mostly of recent introduction and increasingly popular ground-cover roses generally have a compact, spreading habit, forming low, dome-shaped mounds. They look best in informal plantings.

Some are closely allied to rambling species that have a lax habit, and in some cases have inherited their single flowers. These suit a wild garden, combining well with other flowers that have not been heavily hybridized, such as poppies (*Papaver*) and species peonies, such as the excellent *Paeonia mlokosewitschii* (lemon yellow). 'Nozomi' (blush-white), one of the earliest of the type, is still one of the best for this purpose, but there are many more recent introductions that are equally suitable. 'Red Meidiland'

(bright red) is outstanding, and has the advantage of conspicuous hips that redden in autumn.

Ground-cover roses can also be planted to cover banks or cascade over the sides of raised beds. They are equally effective in containers (see Planting a rose in a container) or rockeries. Mulch well in the garden, preferably with bark chippings, not because they are greedier than other types of rose but to help suppress any

MODERN ROSES FOR HEDGING
'Alexander'
'Anne Harkness'
'Chinatown'
'Queen Elizabeth'
'Super Star'

■ BELOW
A weeping standard used to mark the start
of a flight of steps.

Roses with other plants

Mixed planting is now in vogue, with
all types of plant (shrubs, herbaceous
perennials, bulbs and annuals) being
grown together to make an informal
scheme providing pleasure over a long
season. Such a mix also attracts a
wide range of beneficial insects. Roses
are prime candidates for the mixed
border, but note that they are best
kept at a distance from other greedy
shrubs and trees which may compete
for moisture and nutrients (see
Cultivation and planting).

Certain shrubs make dramatic
backdrops. The dense, blackish-green
of a yew hedge looks good with
roses of any colouring, but more
adventurous gardeners might prefer
the grey-green *Eucalyptus gunnii* or,
more dramatically, a purple-leaved
form of *Berberis thunbergii* or *Cotinus
coggygria*, sensational behind a vivid
orange rose such as 'Whisky Mac'.
Cut these shrubs back hard annually
for the best foliage effect.

For an old world look, mix your
roses with any of the traditional
cottage-garden herbaceous plants.
Lupins (*Lupinus*), Canterbury bells
(*Campanula medium*) or foxgloves
(*Digitalis*) will provide strong
verticals, while frothy yellow-green

lady's mantle (*Alchemilla mollis*) or
bronze fennel (*Foeniculum vulgare*
'Purpureum') are marvellous fillers.
Additionally, try the larger, striking
alliums with their spherical heads of
almost geometric precision. For a
slightly more informal look in your
garden, opt for Peruvian lilies
(*Alstroemeria ligtu* hybrids) or day
lilies (*Hemerocallis*), both of which
now have an extended range of
cultivars in a variety of colours.

Since modern roses flower for
several months, you will need a
few late-flowering accompanying
perennials such as anemones,

■ RIGHT
This scheme combines a large-flowered rose with *Geum* 'Mrs Bradshaw', *Lychnis chalcedonica* and *Valeriana officinalis.*

crocosmias or cannas. Some tender perennials also have a comparably long flowering season, notably osteospermums and the blue *Felicia amelloides.* Half-hardy annuals such as tobacco plants (*Nicotiana*) also combine well with roses, as does the Texan bluebell (*Eustoma grandiflorum*). To maintain the display until the first frosts, make sowings throughout the spring. For a jungle-like effect, let a late-flowering clematis – a texensis or viticella type such as 'Gravetye Beauty' (crimson red) or 'Minuet' (white) – wander

■ BELOW
'Iceberg' planted *en masse* with pinks *(Dianthus)* and hardy geraniums.

through neighbouring plants. Cut back hard annually when you prune the roses (see Pruning).

For a vibrant colour scheme, mix the rich amber-yellow 'Glenfiddich' or vermilion 'Alexander' with a red hot poker such as *Kniphofia* 'Prince Igor' (orange-red), and the aptly named *Crocosmia* 'Lucifer' (red). *Hemerocallis* 'Scarlet Orbit' could complete the picture, with annual orange nasturtiums at their feet. You can easily tone down this lively colour scheme with grey-leaved lambs' ears (*Stachys byzantina*), the grey curry plant (*Helichrysum italicum* subsp. *serotinum*) or one of the artemisias.

For an altogether gentler scheme, try the queen of foliage plants, the hosta. Roses with pink in their colouring look best with glaucous hostas such as *H. sieboldiana* 'Elegans' or 'Frances Williams', while the

■ RIGHT
'Amber Queen' planted to echo the
shape of classical columns.

yellows and reds mix well with the
brighter 'Sum and Substance' or
'August Moon'. Subtly coloured
carnations and pinks (*Dianthus*) also
blend well with roses, and have the
advantage of attractive foliage.

There are many excellent modern
roses for the scented garden. Create
an even richer fragrance by stirring in
the delicious *Lilium regale* and annual
tobacco plants, Dame's violet
(*Hesperis matronalis*), mignonette
(*Reseda odorata*) and sweet peas
(*Lathyrus odoratus*). A large mock
orange (*Philadelphus*) will make a
glorious scented backdrop.

MODERN ROSES GROWN FOR THEIR SCENT

'Alec's Red'	'Fragrant Cloud'
'Alexander'	'Helen Traubel'
'Apricot Nectar'	'Ingrid Bergman'
'Arthur Bell'	'Josephine Bruce'
'Betty Prior'	'Lady Hillingdon'
'Blue Moon	'Margaret Merril'
'Bobby Charlton'	'Mister Lincoln'
'Crimson Glory'	'Red Devil'
'Double Delight'	'Royal William'
'Dutch Gold'	'Sheila's Perfume'
'Elizabeth Harkness'	'Sutter's Gold'
'English Miss'	'Whisky Mac'
'Escapade'	'Yesterday'

Roses in containers

With the trend towards ever smaller
gardens, rose breeders have turned
towards dwarf, more compact roses
that can be grown in containers.
Some are no more than 30cm (1ft)
high. You can grow them individually
or make the rose the centrepiece of a
large container, surrounding it with
ivies (*Hedera*), trailing lobelia or the
tender *Lotus berthelotii* (orange-red
to scarlet) and *Helichrysum petiolare*.
The tiniest roses can be planted in
hanging baskets, some of the smaller
ground-cover types with trailing
stems being particularly effective.

Classification and garden use

Rose classification is not an exact science. While the groups are apparently precisely defined horticulturally, such is the diversity of the rose that some exhibit characteristics of more than one group. The groupings are devised for the convenience of the gardener, and are of small significance botanically.

For example, some cluster-flowered roses (e.g. 'Chinatown') are potentially large bushes that some growers prefer to define as shrub roses and treat accordingly. Some large-flowered roses have a tendency to produce smaller buds around the main bud (see Roses as cut flowers: disbudding), showing some of the characteristics of a cluster-flowered rose.

The roses described in this book are deciduous shrubs that bear their flowers on wood produced during the

■ LEFT
Ground-cover roses such as 'Red Bells' have a low, spreading habit and form dome-like mounds.

current season, and on shoots emerging from the previous year's wood. In warm climates roses will grow and flower virtually continuously, but in cold climates they have a period of winter dormancy. They generally benefit from pruning when dormant to maintain a high proportion of young,

productive growth (see Pruning).

Most modern roses are many-petalled. Single flowers have 4–7 petals, semi-double ones have 8–20, double kinds have 20 or more, and fully double ones have 30 and over. Owing to the double nature of most rose flowers and the sterility (or part-sterility) of many, pollination in the

■ LEFT
Large-flowered roses produce their flowers singly at the ends of stems.

■ RIGHT
Cluster-flowered roses produce heads of several blooms.

garden seldom takes place, and hips are not produced.

Modern roses have stronger, richer colours than old roses, and thicker petals that are generally more rain-resistant. They also have a longer flowering season, either in two distinct flushes (one around mid-summer, the other in later summer to autumn) or flowering more or less continuously from summer until the first frosts. Modern roses are usually classified as follows.

Cluster-flowered roses

Sometimes large shrubs that bear single to fully double flowers in clusters. The flowers usually open flat to reveal their stamens, producing dome-shaped heads. Cluster-flowered roses are a diverse group: some can be grown as hedges or as specimens, while others are suitable for bedding or more informal schemes. They are sometimes referred to as floribundas.

Dwarf cluster-flowered bush roses (Patio roses)

Similar in style to cluster-flowered roses, but much smaller. They were bred specifically to be grown in containers, but are also suitable for borders and low hedges.

Ground-cover roses

Roses with a lax, trailing habit, closely allied to ramblers but generally much smaller. Many have single flowers. Ground-cover roses can be used to cover banks, or trail from raised beds. They are sometimes available as weeping standards.

Large-flowered roses

Shrubs characterized by large flowers carried singly (or sometimes in small clusters) that open from pointed buds usually to a high-centred, round or urn-shaped flower. Typically, the flowers are fully double, though there are a few varieties with single flowers. Many are suitable for bedding or mixed planting; a few are stiff, gaunt plants that are best grown solely for cut flowers. Large-flowered roses were formerly referred to as hybrid teas.

Miniature roses

Compact plants, usually under 30cm (1ft) high, with sprays of tiny, usually scentless flowers. Miniature roses can be grown in containers, to edge a border, or in a rock garden. They are sometimes sold as pot plants.

Rugosa roses

A small group, now gaining in popularity, descended from *R. rugosa*. They have characteristically wrinkled leaves and single to double flowers. They tolerate some shade. Rugosas can be used as hedging, as specimens, in the border, or in light woodland.

■ ABOVE
**Fully double flowers have
30 or more petals.**

■ ABOVE
**Semi-double flowers open flat to reveal
their stamens.**

In the following section, roses are arranged according to the following categories: cluster-flowered, dwarf cluster-flowered and miniature, ground-cover, large-flowered and rugosa roses.

Heights and spreads are what the rose can be expected to achieve given good growing conditions. They may vary depending on climate, season and soil types.

Cluster-flowered roses

■ RIGHT

'AMBER QUEEN'

(syn. 'Harroony', 'Prinz Eugen van Savoyen')
Cluster-flowered rose, of neat habit, introduced in 1984. During summer and autumn, it produces clusters of fully double, heavily scented, rich amber-yellow flowers that open from rounded buds. The leaves are tinged red on emergence. Height and spread 50cm (20in). Good for bedding and hedges, 'Amber Queen' is also an outstanding choice for a container.

■ RIGHT

'APRICOT NECTAR'

Cluster-flowered rose, of bushy habit, introduced in 1965. From summer to autumn, it produces tight clusters of large, fully double, sweetly scented, pinkish buff-apricot flowers. The leaves are rounded. Height 80cm (32in), spread 65cm (26in). 'Apricot Nectar' is suitable for a hedge; mildew can be a problem in some areas.

■ RIGHT
'ANNE HARKNESS'

(syn. 'Harkaramel')
Cluster-flowered rose, of upright, branching habit, introduced in 1980. The pointed, urn-shaped, double, soft buff-yellow flowers are borne in large clusters from late summer to autumn. The leaves are mid-green. Height 1.2m (4ft), spread 60cm (2ft). Spectacular in full flower, 'Anne Harkness' is a disease-resistant rose that is suitable for bedding, hedging and cutting.

■ BELOW
'ARTHUR BELL'

Cluster-flowered rose, of upright, branching habit, introduced in 1965. From summer to autumn, it produces clusters of semi-double to double, strongly scented, bright yellow flowers that pale as they age. The leaves are leathery and glossy. Height to 90cm (3ft), spread 60cm (2ft). 'Arthur Bell' is a versatile rose, suitable for bedding, hedging and containers; the autumn flowering is especially good.

■ FAR LEFT
'CHINATOWN'

(syn. 'Ville de Chine')
Cluster-flowered rose, of bushy, upright
habit, introduced in 1963. Clusters of fully
double, fragrant, bright golden-yellow
flowers are freely produced throughout the
summer into autumn. The leaves are glossy
dark green. Height 1.5m (5ft), spread
90cm (3ft). One of the largest of its type,
'Chinatown' can be grown at the back
of a border, as a hedge or specimen.

■ ABOVE RIGHT
'ELIZABETH OF GLAMIS'

(syn. 'Irish Beauty')
Cluster-flowered rose, of upright habit,
introduced in 1964. Clusters of double,
sweetly scented, soft salmon-pink flowers
are carried throughout the summer and
autumn. The leaves are dark green and
semi-glossy. Height 75cm (2½ft), spread
60cm (2ft). 'Elizabeth of Glamis' is an
outstanding rose of its type and has stood
the test of time; however, it does not
always thrive on cold, heavy soils.

■ LEFT
'CIRCUS'

Cluster-flowered rose, of upright,
branching habit, introduced in 1956.
Throughout the summer, clusters of
yellow buds open to shapely, cupped, fully
double, slightly fragrant flowers with
orange-yellow petals suffused with pink.
The leaves are glossy dark green. Height
75cm (2½ft), spread 60cm (2ft). 'Circus',
though of unique colouring, has lost some
of its former popularity because of its
susceptibility to disease.

■ ABOVE LEFT
'ESCAPADE'

(syn. 'Harpade')
Cluster-flowered rose, of freely branching habit, introduced in
1967. The semi-double, sweetly scented flowers are of unique
colouring: borne in clusters from summer to autumn, they are soft
lilac-pink, opening flat to reveal white centres and golden stamens.
The leaves are glossy bright green. Height to 1.2m (4ft), spread
60cm (2ft). A disease-resistant rose, 'Escapade' is good for cutting
and in mixed plantings; it occasionally produces pure white
flowers within the cluster.

■ ABOVE RIGHT
'HANNAH GORDON'

(syn. 'Korweiso', 'Raspberry Ice')
Cluster-flowered rose, of spreading, open habit, introduced in
1983. In summer and autumn, it produces clusters of lightly
scented, double flowers that have creamy pink petals shading
to deeper pink at the edges. The leaves are glossy dark green.
Height 80cm (32in), spread 65cm (26in). 'Hannah Gordon',
a disease-resistant rose, is good for cutting and can also be
grown in a container.

■ LEFT
'EYE PAINT'

(syn. 'Maceyc', 'Tapis Persan')
Cluster-flowered rose, of bushy, free-branching habit,
introduced in 1975. Large clusters of single, lightly scented
flowers cover the bush during summer and autumn; bright
scarlet, they open flat to reveal white centres and golden
stamens. Height to 1.2m (4ft), spread 75cm (2½ft). 'Eye
Paint' does best with light pruning and makes a good hedge;
deadhead regularly to maintain the flowering performance.

■ RIGHT

'ICEBERG'

(syn. 'Fée des Neiges', 'Korbin',
'Schneewittchen')
Cluster-flowered rose, of elegant, branching
habit, introduced in 1958. From summer
to autumn, clusters of double, ivory-white,
lightly scented flowers, carried in abundance,
open from tapering, pink-flushed buds.
The leaves are glossy bright green. Height
to 1.5m (5ft), spread to 90cm (3ft) or more.
An outstanding rose of its type, 'Iceberg'
can be used for bedding, hedging, cutting
or, with minimum pruning, as a specimen.

■ LEFT

'KORRESIA'

(syn. 'Friesia',
'Sunsprite')
Cluster-flowered
rose, of neat,
upright habit,
introduced in 1974.
From summer to
autumn, clusters of
shapely buds open
to double, fragrant,
bright golden-
yellow flowers that
hold their colour
well. The leaves are
glossy light green.
Height 75cm
(2½ft), spread 60cm
(2ft). 'Korresia' can
be used for bedding
and to provide cut
flowers; it is similar
to 'Allgold' but has
bigger flowers.

■ ABOVE LEFT
'LILLI MARLENE'

Cluster-flowered rose, of slender, branching habit, introduced in 1959. Large clusters of double, only lightly scented, deep rich crimson flowers are produced from summer to autumn on plum-red shoots. The leaves are glossy dark green, tinted red on emergence. Height 70cm (28in), spread 60cm (2ft). 'Lilli Marlene' is tolerant of both rain and hot sun, and makes a good hedge.

■ ABOVE RIGHT
'MASQUERADE'

Cluster-flowered rose, of compact habit, introduced in 1949. From summer to autumn, clusters of yellow buds open to semi-double, only lightly scented, salmon-pink flowers that age to deep red, with all colours present simultaneously. The leaves are glossy dark green. Height 90cm (3ft), spread 75cm (2½ft). 'Masquerade' makes an excellent hedge; deadhead regularly to maintain flowering.

■ ABOVE
'MARGARET MERRIL'

(syn. 'Harkuly')
Cluster-flowered rose, of upright habit, introduced in 1977. Clusters of large, shapely, double, sweetly scented, pure white flowers are carried from summer to autumn. The leaves are glossy dark green. Height 90cm (3ft), spread 60cm (2ft). Besides its versatility in the garden, 'Margaret Merril' can also be grown in containers and used as a cut flower, but blackspot can be a problem.

■ ABOVE LEFT
'MOUNTBATTEN'

(syn. 'Harmantelle')
Cluster-flowered rose, of dense, upright habit, introduced in 1982.
Small clusters of large, double, lightly scented, mimosa-yellow
flowers are carried from summer to autumn. The leaves are glossy
dark green. Height to 1.5m (5ft), spread to 90cm (3ft). A vigorous
rose that, with minimum pruning, makes an excellent specimen.

■ ABOVE RIGHT
'QUEEN ELIZABETH'

(syn. 'The Queen Elizabeth Rose')
Cluster-flowered rose, of strongly upright habit, introduced in
1954. From summer to autumn, it produces clusters of large, fully
double, only lightly scented, deep china-pink flowers. The leaves
are glossy dark green. Height to 2m (6½ft) or more, spread 90cm
(3ft). 'Queen Elizabeth' is an outstanding rose but can be difficult
to place in the garden: use it at the back of a border or as a hedge.
The flowers last well when cut.

■ LEFT
'SEXY REXY'

(syn. 'Heckenzauber', 'Macrexy')
Cluster-flowered rose, of upright habit, introduced in 1984. Clusters
of shapely, fully double, lightly scented, clear light pink flowers are
produced in summer and autumn. The leaves are glossy dark green.
Height and spread 60cm (2ft). A versatile rose, 'Sexy Rexy' is good
for garden use, in containers, and as a cut flower.

■ ABOVE
'SHEILA'S PERFUME'

(syn. 'Harsherry')
Cluster-flowered rose, of upright habit,
introduced in 1985. The flowers, carried
singly and in clusters from summer to
autumn, are double and sweetly scented;
the petals are yellow marked with red,
fading to pink. The leaves are glossy dark
green. Height 75cm (2½ft), spread 60cm
(2ft). 'Sheila's Perfume' makes an excellent
low hedge, grows well in containers, and
provides good cut flowers.

■ ABOVE RIGHT
'THE FAIRY'

Cluster-flowered rose, usually classified
as a polyantha, of dense, mounding habit,
introduced in 1932. From late summer
to late autumn, clusters of small, double,
virtually scentless, light pink flowers
appear in profusion. The leaves are
glossy mid-green. Height and spread
60cm (2ft) or more. A dainty rose,
'The Fairy' is valued principally for
its late flowering season.

■ LEFT
'YESTERDAY'

(syn. 'Tapis
d'Orient')
Cluster-flowered rose,
usually classified as a
polyantha, of elegant,
open, spreading habit,
introduced in 1974.
From summer to
autumn, clusters of
semi-double, fragrant,
deep lilac-pink
flowers, produced in
succession, open flat
to reveal paler centres
and golden stamens.
The leaves are glossy
dark green. Height
and spread 90cm (3ft)
or more. 'Yesterday'
has any number of
uses in the garden
and provides good
cut flowers; with light
pruning, it makes an
attractive specimen.

Dwarf cluster-flowered and miniature roses

■ ABOVE LEFT
'ANNA FORD'

(syn. 'Harpiccolo')
Dwarf cluster-flowered rose, of dense, low, free-branching habit,
introduced in 1981. The warm orange-red flowers, produced freely
from summer to autumn, open flat from pointed buds to reveal
yellow centres. The leaves are glossy dark green. Height 45cm
(1½ft), spread 38cm (15in). 'Anna Ford' was one of the first of
its type and is still popular as a bedding or container rose.

■ ABOVE RIGHT
'BABY MASQUERADE'

(syn. 'Baby Carnival', 'Tanba', 'Tanbakede')
Miniature rose, of upright, bushy habit, introduced in 1956.
From summer to autumn, it carries clusters of tiny, double flowers
that open yellow and fade to pink, then deeper red. The plentiful
leaves are dark green. Height and spread 40cm (16in). A healthy
rose, 'Baby Masquerade' can be used for bedding; it is widely
available as a standard.

■ LEFT
'CINDERELLA'

Miniature rose, of upright,
bushy habit, introduced
in 1952. Clusters of fully
double, only lightly
scented, blush-pink flowers
are produced in abundance
from summer to autumn.
The tiny leaves are pointed
and glossy. Height and
spread to 25cm (10in).
An outstanding miniature,
'Cinderella' is virtually
unique of its type because
it is best with some shade.

■ RIGHT
'QUEEN MOTHER'

(syn. 'Korquemu')
Dwarf cluster-flowered rose, of spreading habit, introduced in 1991. The semi-double, only lightly scented, clear pink flowers are produced from summer to autumn. The leaves are small and glossy. Height 45cm (1½ft), spread 60cm (2ft). 'Queen Mother' can be used as ground cover and is excellent in a container; it is sometimes available as a weeping standard.

■ ABOVE LEFT
'RISE 'N' SHINE'

(syn. 'Golden Meillandina', 'Golden Sunblaze')
Miniature rose, of upright, branching habit, introduced in 1977. From summer to autumn, clusters of fully double, virtually scentless, deep yellow flowers are borne. The leaves are small and pointed. Height 45cm (1½ft), spread 40cm (16in). 'Rise 'n' Shine' is one of the best miniature yellow roses and is good for cutting.

■ ABOVE RIGHT
'SWEET DREAM'

(syn. 'Fryminicot')
Dwarf cluster-flowered rose, of stiffly upright habit, introduced in 1988. From summer to autumn, it produces an abundance of fully double, lightly scented, soft apricot-orange flowers. The leaves are matt dark green. Height 40cm (16in), spread 35cm (14in). An outstanding rose of its type, 'Sweet Dream' can be used for low hedging or to edge a border.

Ground-cover roses

'AVON'

(syn. 'Fairy Lights',
'Poulmulti',
'Sunnyside')
Ground-cover rose, of
low, compact, spreading
habit, introduced in
1992. From summer to
autumn, clusters of small,
semi-double, fragrant,
pinkish-white flowers
open flat to reveal golden
stamens. The leaves are
glossy mid-green. Height
30cm (1ft), spread 90cm
(3ft). Besides making
excellent ground cover,
'Avon' can also be grown
successfully in containers.

■ RIGHT
'WHITE FLOWER CARPET'

(syn. 'Heidetraum', 'Noatraum')
Ground-cover rose, of spreading habit,
introduced in 1991. From summer to
autumn, and sometimes later, it produces
clusters of small, double, only lightly
scented, pure white flowers. The leaves are
glossy. Height 75cm (2½ft), spread 1.2m
(4ft). Aptly named, 'White Flower Carpet'
can be used to cover a bank, or grown
in containers.

Large-flowered roses

■ ABOVE
'ALEXANDER'

(syn. 'Alexandra')
Large-flowered rose, of upright habit, introduced in 1972.
The double, luminous red flowers open from pointed buds
from summer to autumn. The leaves are glossy dark green.
Height to 2m (6½ft), spread 75cm (2½ft). 'Alexander',
a disease-resistant rose, bears its flowers on long stems
that make them particularly suitable for cutting.

■ ABOVE
'ALEC'S RED'

(syn. 'Cored')
Large-flowered rose, of bushy habit, introduced in 1970. Large,
fully double, heavily scented, rich red flowers open from pointed
buds throughout summer and into autumn. The leaves are dark
green. Height 90cm (3ft), spread 60cm (2ft). 'Alec's Red' is a
versatile rose, suitable for cutting, bedding, and as a hedge.

■ RIGHT
'BIG PURPLE'

(syn. 'Nuit d'Orient', 'Stebigpu', 'Stephens' Big Purple')
Large-flowered rose, of upright habit, introduced in 1987.
The large, rich purplish-red flowers are fully double and heavily
scented, appearing from summer to autumn. The leaves are
dark green. Height 90cm (3ft), spread 60cm (2ft). 'Big Purple',
of almost unique colouring, is good for bedding and cutting.

■ ABOVE LEFT

'BLUE MOON'

(syn. 'Blue Monday', 'Mainzer Fastnacht', 'Sissi',
'Tannacht')
Large-flowered rose, of upright, branching habit, introduced in
1964. In summer and autumn, shapely, fully double, silvery lilac
flowers that are sweetly scented are carried in abundance. The
leaves are large and dark green. Height 90cm (3ft), spread 60cm
(2ft). Generally considered to be the best "blue" rose, 'Blue Moon'
needs careful placing in the garden because of its curious colouring;
it is perhaps best grown under glass.

■ ABOVE RIGHT

'BOBBY CHARLTON'

Large-flowered rose, of upright habit, introduced in 1974.
It produces high-centred, fully double, scented, soft pink flowers
from late summer to autumn. The large leaves are dark green and
semi-glossy. Height 90cm (3ft), spread 60cm (2ft). Generally
a healthy rose, 'Bobby Charlton' performs well in wet weather
and is a good choice for exhibition.

■ RIGHT
'CHRYSLER IMPERIAL'

Large-flowered rose, of neat, upright habit,
introduced in 1952. The very fragrant,
fully double, vivid red flowers open from
pointed buds then fade to dull purplish-
red. The leaves are dark green. Height
90cm (3ft), spread 60cm (2ft). 'Chrysler
Imperial' is grown exclusively for the
perfection of individual flowers and is
a good rose for exhibition if disbudded;
its propensity to disease makes it a poor
choice for other purposes.

■ BELOW RIGHT
'DOUBLE DELIGHT'

(syn. 'Andeli')
Large-flowered rose, of freely branching
habit, introduced in 1977. From summer
to autumn, it produces large, shapely, fully
double, sweetly scented flowers that have
creamy-white petals flushed cherry-red
at the edges. The leaves are semi-glossy.
Height 90cm (3ft), spread 60cm (2ft).
'Double Delight' is an outstanding rose
that is good for bedding and cutting,
though the flowers can be spoilt by rain.

■ OPPOSITE BELOW
'CHICAGO PEACE'

Large-flowered rose, of bushy, spreading
habit, introduced in 1962. The huge, only
lightly scented flowers, produced from
summer to autumn, have coppery pink
petals with a yellow reverse. The leaves are
glossy dark green. Height to 1.5m (5ft),
spread 90cm (3ft). 'Chicago Peace', a sport
(spontaneous mutation) of 'Peace', can be
used as a specimen if pruned only lightly;
otherwise, use it for bedding or hedging.

■ ABOVE LEFT
'DUTCH GOLD'

Large-flowered rose, of upright habit, introduced in
1978. The shapely, fully double, bright golden-yellow
flowers, carried from summer to autumn, are sweetly
scented. The leaves are glossy dark green. Height 90cm
(3ft), spread 60cm (2ft). 'Dutch Gold' is an excellent
bedding rose; the flowers hold their colour well.

■ ABOVE RIGHT
'ELINA'

(syn. 'Dicjana', 'Peaudouce')
Large-flowered rose, of bushy habit, introduced in
1985. During summer and autumn, fully double,
lightly scented, creamy white flowers open to reveal
lemon-yellow flushed centres. The leaves are tinted red.
Height 90cm (3ft), spread 75cm (2½ft). 'Elina' is a
versatile rose that is easy to grow; generally healthy,
it can be used for bedding and cutting.

■ LEFT
'ELIZABETH HARKNESS'

Large-flowered rose, of upright habit, introduced in
1969. From summer to autumn, it produces shapely,
fully double, fragrant, ivory-white flowers that flush
pink as they age. The leaves are semi-glossy. Height
75cm (2½ft), spread 60cm (2ft). 'Elizabeth Harkness'
is good for cutting and bedding; the flowers are of
perfect form but can be spoilt by wet weather.

■ LEFT

'FRAGRANT CLOUD'

(syn. 'Duftwolke',
'Nuage Parfum',
'Tanellis')
Large-flowered rose, of
sturdy, branching habit,
introduced in 1963. The
large, fully double, richly
scented, bright geranium-
red flowers, ageing to
purplish-red, are carried
from summer to autumn.
The leaves are leathery and
dark green. Height 75cm
(2½ft), spread 60cm (2ft).
'Fragrant Cloud' is an
outstanding rose that can
be used for bedding or
cutting; the fragrance
is virtually unsurpassed
among modern roses.

■ RIGHT

'GRANDPA DICKSON'

(syn. 'Irish Gold')
Large-flowered rose, of very upright habit, introduced
in 1966. Large, double, only lightly scented flowers,
freely borne from summer to autumn, are soft pale
yellow, occasionally flushed with pink. The leaves are
small and light green. Height 75cm (2½ft), spread
60cm (2ft). Its disease resistance and tolerance
of rough weather make 'Grandpa Dickson'
an outstanding bedding rose; for top quality
performance good cultivation is essential.

■ ABOVE LEFT
'INGRID BERGMAN'

(syn. 'Poulman')
Large-flowered rose, of upright, branching habit, introduced in 1984. The fully double, only lightly scented, deep red flowers are carried from summer to autumn. The leaves are glossy dark green. Height 75cm (2½ft), spread 60cm (2ft). Good for cutting, bedding and containers, 'Ingrid Bergman' is one of the best in its colour range.

■ ABOVE RIGHT
'JULIA'S ROSE'

Large-flowered rose, of upright but spindly habit, introduced in 1976. The shapely, double, urn-shaped flowers, produced from summer to autumn, are of unique colouring: the petals are coppery bronze to buff, shaded brownish-pink. The leaves are reddish-green and sparse. Height 75cm (2½ft), spread 45cm (1½ft). Despite its weak growth, 'Julia's Rose' is worth growing for the beauty of the individual flowers.

■ RIGHT
'KING'S RANSOM'

Large-flowered rose, of branching habit,
introduced in 1961. From summer to
autumn, it bears a profusion of fully
double, lightly scented, pure yellow
flowers. The leaves are glossy dark green.
Height 75cm (2½ft), spread 60cm (2ft).
'King's Ransom' is excellent for bedding
and as a cut flower, but does not do well
on light, chalky (alkaline) soils.

■ RIGHT
'MISTER LINCOLN'

Large-flowered rose, of upright habit,
introduced in 1964. Fully double, very
fragrant, deep dusky-red flowers are
produced in summer and autumn.
The leaves are matt dark green. Height to
1.2m (4ft), spread to 90cm (3ft). 'Mister
Lincoln' is excellent for cutting, but tends
to produce its flowers in clusters; disbud
for prime quality blooms.

■ OPPOSITE BELOW
'JUST JOEY'

Large-flowered rose, of upright, branching
habit, introduced in 1973. Elegant, long,
shapely buds open to lightly scented, fully
double, coppery orange-pink flowers with
slightly ruffled petals. The matt dark green
leaves are tinted red on emergence. Height
75cm (2½ft), spread 60cm (2ft). 'Just Joey'
is an outstanding rose, valued for its
freedom of flowering, general disease-
resistance and versatility in the garden,
besides the unusual colour of the blooms.

■ RIGHT
'OLYMPIAD'

(syn. 'Macauck')
Large-flowered rose,
of upright, bushy
habit, introduced
in 1984. The
fully double, only
lightly scented,
bright red flowers
are produced from
summer to autumn.
The leaves are
matt mid-green.
Height 1.2m (4ft),
spread 60cm (2ft).
'Olympiad' is an
excellent rose
for cutting.

■ BELOW LEFT
'PAPA MEILLAND'

(syn. 'Meisar')
Large-flowered rose, of upright habit,
introduced in 1963. From summer to
autumn, it produces shapely, fully double,
strongly fragrant, deep crimson flowers.
The leaves are glossy dark green. Height
90cm (3ft), spread 60cm (2ft). Excellent
as a cut flower, 'Papa Meilland' is grown
for the beauty of the individual blooms;
on the debit side, flowering is not profuse,
and the plant is prone to disease.

■ BELOW RIGHT
'PASCALI'

Large-flowered rose, of upright, open
habit, introduced in 1963. Throughout
summer and autumn, it produces shapely,
double, only lightly scented flowers that
have white petals shaded creamy buff.
The leaves are glossy dark green, but
sparse. Height 90cm (3ft), spread 75cm
(2½ft). The flowers of 'Pascali' show
unsurpassed rain-resistance; they are
exceptionally long-lasting when cut.

■ RIGHT
'PAUL
SHIRVILLE'

(syn.
'Harqueterwife',
'Heart Throb')
Large-flowered rose,
of slightly spreading
habit, introduced in
1983. The double,
fragrant, warm pink
flowers are carried
from summer to
autumn. The leaves
are large and dark
green. Height 90cm
(3ft), spread 75cm
(2½ft). 'Paul
Shirville' tolerates
poor soil and is
good for bedding
and containers.

■ LEFT
'PEACE'

(syn. 'Gioia', 'Gloria Dei', 'Mme A.
Meilland')
Large-flowered rose, of spreading, bushy
habit, bred in 1942. The large, fully
double, only lightly scented flowers are
pale yellow with pink flushes, and appear
from mid-summer to autumn. The leaves
are glossy dark green. Height to 1.5m (5ft)
or more, spread 90cm (3ft) or more. One
of the most popular and best-known roses
ever bred, 'Peace' is a vigorous plant that
makes a fine specimen with light pruning.

■ OPPOSITE TOP
'ROYAL WILLIAM'

(syn. 'Duftzauber '84', 'Fragrant
Charm '84', 'Korzaun')
Large-flowered rose, of upright habit,
introduced in 1984. From summer to
autumn, it carries large, fully double,
fragrant, deep crimson flowers on long
stems. The leaves are glossy dark green.
Height 90cm (3ft), spread 75cm (2½ft).
'Royal William' is good for bedding and
excellent for cutting.

■ BELOW
'RED DEVIL'

(syn. 'Coeur d'Amour')
Large-flowered rose, of bushy habit,
introduced in 1967. From summer to
autumn, it produces large, shapely, fully
double, fragrant, vivid scarlet flowers.
The leaves are glossy dark green. Height
90cm (3ft), spread 75cm (2½ft). 'Red
Devil' is splendid for exhibition; it is
also a good bedding rose, though the
flowers can be spoilt by rain.

■ ABOVE
'PICCADILLY'

Large-flowered rose, of upright, branching habit,
introduced in 1959. From summer to autumn, it produces
double, only lightly scented flowers with bright scarlet
petals with a yellow reverse ageing to orange. The leaves
are glossy dark green, tinged bronze. Height 90cm (3ft),
spread 60cm (2ft). 'Piccadilly' performs best in cool
weather, bright sunlight turning the colour a more
uniform orange; blackspot can be a problem.

■ BELOW LEFT
'SAVOY HOTEL'

(syn. 'Harvintage', 'Integrity')
Large-flowered rose, of bushy habit, introduced
in 1989. From summer to autumn, strong stems
carry large, shapely, fully double, fragrant, light
clear pink flowers. The leaves are dark green.
Height 90cm (3ft), spread 60cm (2ft). 'Savoy
Hotel' is a versatile rose that provides excellent
material for cutting; it needs good cultivation
for top-rate performance.

■ BELOW RIGHT
'SUPER STAR'

(syn. 'Tanorstar', 'Tropicana')
Large-flowered rose, of branching but uneven
habit, introduced in 1960. The large, shapely,
double, lightly scented, luminous vermilion
flowers are produced from summer to autumn.
The leaves are semi-glossy. Height and spread
90cm (3ft). 'Super Star' is grown for the beauty
of individual blooms and is difficult to place in
a mixed border; it can be susceptible to mildew.

■ BELOW
'WHISKY MAC'

(syn. 'Tanky', 'Whisky')
Large-flowered rose, of upright, bushy
habit, introduced in 1967. From summer
to autumn, it produces an abundance of
large, fully double, strongly fragrant, rich
amber-yellow flowers. The leaves are glossy
dark green. Height 75cm (2½ft), spread
60cm (2ft). Despite sometimes suffering
from dieback and fungal diseases, 'Whisky
Mac' retains its popularity because of its
unique flower colour.

■ ABOVE
'TROIKA'

(syn. 'Royal Dane')
Large-flowered rose, of upright, branching habit,
introduced in 1972. From summer to autumn, it produces
large, shapely, double, lightly scented, copper-orange
flowers that are sometimes veined scarlet. The leaves are
glossy dark green. Height 90cm (3ft), spread 75cm (2½ft).
Disease- and weather-resistant, 'Troika' is a good choice
for a massed planting and provides good cut flowers.

Rugosa roses

■ RIGHT
'HANSA'

Rugosa rose, of dense habit, introduced in
1905. Double, very fragrant, reddish-purple
flowers are freely produced throughout the
summer; in autumn, large red hips develop.
The leaves are tough, wrinkled and dark
green. Height 1.2m (4ft), spread 90cm (3ft).
A versatile rose, 'Hansa' can be grown as a
specimen, in light shade, or as a hedge.

■ ABOVE
'ROSERAIE DE L'HAY'

Rugosa rose, of dense, spreading habit, introduced in 1901.
Throughout the summer and into autumn, it produces double,
strongly scented, wine-red flowers that open to reveal creamy
stamens. The wrinkled leaves redden in autumn. Height 2m (6½ft)
or more, spread 1.2m (4ft) or more. 'Roseraie de l'Hay ' makes an
excellent hedge and can also be planted in light shade.

■ ABOVE
'SCHNEEZWERG'

(syn. 'Snow Dwarf')
Rugosa rose, of dense, spreading habit, introduced in 1912.
From late spring until late autumn, it produces anemone-like,
semi-double, only lightly scented, white flowers that open flat
to reveal golden stamens; small orange-red hips follow. The
leaves are greyish-green. Height 1.2m (4ft), spread 1.5m (5ft).
The autumn display of 'Schneezwerg' is particularly good, though
the foliage does not change colour; flowers continue to appear
alongside the reddening hips. For the best fruiting, deadhead
selectively in summer.

■ BELOW
If possible, slide a containerized rose from
its container before buying and check that
the root system is healthy.

The Grower's Guide

Buying roses

Roses are sold as bare-root plants or
in containers. The former are lifted
from the open ground when
dormant, and the roots are shaken
free of soil. They are often sold by
mail order and a huge range is
available, including rare varieties.

Roses sold in containers are lifted
from the field, potted up and grown
on. They are available at garden
centres throughout the growing
season but are more expensive than
bare-root plants. However, they often
establish more quickly.

When buying a containerized rose,
choose one that is growing evenly,

showing no sign of disease or pest
attack. Weed-seedlings on the surface
of the compost (soil mix) are of no
consequence. However, the presence
of moss or lichens suggests
nutrient exhaustion,
or that the plant has
been waterlogged.

If possible, slide the plant
from its container and
check the root system.

If the roots are tightly coiled
around the pot, reject it.
Such plants usually fail to
establish properly.

■ LEFT AND
BELOW
Roses sold in
containers are
usually in full
growth, while
bare-root
roses are sold
while dormant.

Cultivation and planting

Roses will grow in all soil types apart from soil that is permanently waterlogged. It is often stated that roses prefer heavy clay soils, but this is only because clay tends to retain nutrients well. Light, sandy soil will also support roses if improved with organic matter prior to planting.

Roses generally prefer an open site in full sun, with shelter from strong, drying winds. Rugosa roses tolerate some degree of shade, but flowering is less profuse. No rose thrives in deep shade.

Improving the soil

Digging in organic matter greatly improves the texture of all soil, opening up heavy soil that clogs by binding it into crumbs, while aiding water retention on light, sandy ground. On very heavy soils, dig in horticultural grit, at the rate of one bucketful per 1sq m (1sq yd).

Roses benefit from an annual mulch of organic matter in autumn or spring. This improves soil fertility and structure and conserves moisture.

Fertilizers

All roses benefit from additional feeding during the growing season, even if you mulch annually. There are three major elements that are needed in quantity for plant growth. Nitrogen (N) stimulates lush, leafy growth; potassium (K) promotes good flowering and fruiting, and firms the growth; phosphorus (P) aids good root development. Other elements ("trace elements") are also present in the soil in minute

---

SOIL IMPROVERS

Farmyard manure
Manure that has been collected from a farmyard is an excellent soil improver, but you need to make sure that it has been well-rotted, otherwise it may take nitrogen out of the soil as it breaks down. Its nutrient quotient can be low relative to its bulk. Chicken and pigeon manure is high in nitrogen.

Peat
This is light and pleasant to handle, but being inert does not provide any additional nutrients. Nowadays, extensive use of peat is frowned upon, because it is not a renewable resource.

Garden compost
This is the best of all soil improvers, being both friable in texture and high in nutrients. However, it is difficult to make in sufficient quantities to satisfy all your gardening needs.

Grit
This can be used to improve the drainage on very heavy clay soils, but being inert does not provide any nutrients. It can also be used as a mulch, or as a top-dressing for plants in containers.

Leaf mould
Made by allowing fallen leaves (which must be disease-free) to break down, leaf mould is a superb soil improver, being light of texture and virtually weed-free, but takes at least two years to produce.

Spent mushroom compost
This is available from commercial producers, and is an excellent material, fertile and usually weed-free. However, note that it tends to be chalky and should therefore not be added to soils that are already very alkaline.

FERTILIZERS

Bonemeal

This is an organic fertilizer high in phosphorus which breaks down slowly in the soil. Fork it into the soil on planting; use as a top-dressing each autumn. Always wear rubber gloves and a mask when handling bonemeal.

Rose fertilizer

Proprietary rose fertilizers are inorganic and contain all the major elements with a high proportion of potassium. Apply at the start of the growing season, and in summer immediately after the first flush of flowers, to build up the plant's resources for later flowering.

Growmore

This is a balanced (or straight) inorganic fertilizer that contains all the major elements in equal proportions. Use it at the start of the growing season to give the roses a boost, but in place of, not as well as, any other fertilizer.

Pelleted chicken manure

This is an organic fertilizer that is becoming increasingly popular. It is higher in potassium than raw manure.

quantities, but they seldom need to be applied unless you know there is a deficiency.

Organic and inorganic fertilizers are available, some specially formulated for roses. Some are in powder or granular form, to be forked in around the plant; others are liquid feeds applied as a root drench from a watering can or sprayed on as a foliar feed. Foliar feeds are advantageous if you need to give a rose a boost after a disease or pest attack, since the nutrients are immediately available to the plant.

Fertilizers must be applied at the rate recommended by manufacturers.

Planting

Prior to planting, prepare the site by digging it over. Remove all weeds and dig in organic matter. If the soil is very heavy, add grit.

Bare-root roses should be planted as soon after receipt as possible, preferably during a mild spell. If the ground is unworkable because frozen or waterlogged, they can be stored unopened for up to six weeks in a cool, dark, frost-free place. Remove the packaging and cut back any damaged or twiggy growth. Lightly trim the roots, then soak the rose for up to one hour in a bucket of water.

Containerized roses can be planted at any time of year except when the ground is frozen or during periods of drought. If you cannot plant immediately, keep the rose in a sheltered place and water it regularly.

Dig a hole large enough to take the root system comfortably (bare-root), or twice the width and depth of the pot (containerized). Fork in a handful of bonemeal and a little organic matter at the base of the hole. Set the rose in position and check the planting depth. The graft union

■ RIGHT
A bed of standards and bush roses. Plant all roses as soon as possible after receiving them.

PLANTING A CONTAINERIZED STANDARD

1 Choose a well-protected site, then dig a hole about twice the depth and twice the width of the container.

2 Fork bonemeal and garden compost, well-rotted farmyard manure or leaf mould into the base of the hole.

3 Check the planting depth. Plant the rose so that the compost (soil mix) surface is level with the surrounding soil. If planting a bare-root standard, look for the soil mark on the stem which indicates the level of planting in the nursery.

4 Position the rose in the centre of the hole, then drive in a stake just off-centre. Take care not to damage the rose's roots. The stake should come to just below the head of the rose.

5 Slide the rose from its container, and gently tease out some of the roots with a handfork.

6 Set the rose in position and backfill with soil. Firm in the rose lightly.

7 Use ties to fasten the stem of the rose to the stake.

8 With proper care, the rose should flourish, as shown. Water well in the first season to establish the plant.

(where the top-growth meets the rootstock) should be just below soil level. Ease containerized roses out of their pots and gently loosen the roots.

Backfill with the excavated soil. Firm in lightly with your foot, fork a little fertilizer around the base of the plant and water well. Apply a mulch of organic matter in a ring around the base to conserve moisture, and lightly prune the top-growth, if necessary (see Pruning). Water freely during the first season after planting to ensure rapid establishment. In subsequent years, provided you mulch, watering should not be necessary.

Planting standard roses is slightly more involved. Choose a sheltered site. Standard roses are top-heavy and easily blown over or broken by strong winds.

Planting a rose in a container

Many modern roses are suitable for growing in containers. All the miniature and patio roses are good candidates, as are other shorter-growing and less vigorous varieties. Check the expected height and spread of the rose, and choose a container to suit. Heavy stone or unglazed terracotta containers are best. They provide good ballast and are water- and air-permeable, thus reducing the risk of waterlogging. In addition, they are less likely to blow over in strong winds than lightweight plastic vessels. Use lightweight plastic containers only where there is no alternative, on a balcony or roof garden, for instance. They can become waterlogged and tend to overheat in summer.

■ ABOVE
Ground-cover roses can also be very effective in containers: in patios, roof gardens or rockeries.

Roses in containers do best in soil-based composts (soil mixes), preferably John Innes No. 3, which have certain advantages over soilless ones. If allowed to dry out, they are easier to re-wet. They also tend to have a higher nutrient quotient. Where weight is an issue, you can still achieve good results with soilless composts, provided you feed and water the plant regularly.

All roses in containers need regular watering. You will need to water at least once, and probably twice a day at the height of summer. Adding water-retaining gel to the compost can help to reduce the problem.

Supplementary feeding is also necessary. Use a proprietary rose

MODERN ROSES SUITABLE FOR GROWING IN CONTAINERS

Apart from miniature and patio roses, all of which are suitable, the following modern roses can be successfully grown in containers:

'Anisley Dickson'	'Hannah Gordon'
'Amber Queen'	'Ingrid Bergman'
'Arthur Bell'	'King's Ransom'
'Blue Moon'	'Lady Hillingdon'
'Double Delight'	'Margaret Merril'
'Elizabeth Harkness'	'Precious Platinum'
'English Miss'	'Princess Michael of Kent'
	'Sexy Rexy'
	'Sheila's Perfume'
	'Southampton'
	'Tango'

1 Cover the base of the container with crocks, stones or rubble to facilitate drainage and add stability.

2 Begin to fill with compost (soil mix).

3 For improved drainage, replace up to a third of the compost with grit. You can also mix in garden compost or leaf mould.

4 When about half full, set the rose in the middle of the container and check the planting depth. You need to cover the graft union of the rose, and provide a gap of about 2.5cm (1in) between the compost surface and the edge of the pot, to allow for watering.

5 Ease the rose from its pot, and fork over the rootball gently to tease out some of the roots. This will accelerate establishment.

6 Backfill with more compost.

7 Incorporate some slow-release fertilizer pellets, according to the manufacturer's instructions.

8 Water in well and top-dress with a layer of grit. Properly cared for, the rose will flower freely.

fertilizer or a liquid feed, or pelleted fertilizer for plants in containers. Keep the compost weed-free.

Plants in containers are vulnerable to sudden changes in temperature. The roots can bake in summer on a hard, concrete surface that reflects heat so some shade from the hot mid-day sun may be necessary. In winter, the compost can freeze solid. Either move pots into a sheltered spot, or wrap them loosely in hessian (burlap).

Roses will flourish in the same container for several years. Refresh compost annually by tilting the pot and scraping away the top layer, replacing it with new compost. After a few years' growth, remove the plant entirely and shake the roots free. Wash the container, trim the roots, and replant with fresh compost.

Pruning

Pruning a rose refreshes the plant and maintains an open, vase-shaped habit. It also promotes free air circulation through the plant, minimizing the risk of mildew and other fungal diseases (see Pests, diseases and other disorders). There are no set rules for pruning. Be guided by your own judgement and the way the rose is growing. Very vigorous roses often achieve their true potential only when left mostly to their own devices. Conversely, some weak-growing roses benefit from regular hard pruning.

Bear in mind a few basic principles. Pruning always stimulates vigorous new growth, which arises from the growth bud nearest to the cut. To promote even, balanced growth, prune straggly, weak stems

■ ABOVE
Cut out all dead, diseased and damaged wood.

hard but trim vigorous stems only lightly. If in doubt, prune lightly. You can always prune again later. Roses are forgiving plants: provided you feed and mulch well after pruning you are unlikely to do any lasting harm to the plant whatever your pruning strategy.

Timing

When you prune your roses is a matter of judgement, depending to some extent on the local climate. In principle, you can prune at any time when the rose is dormant, from late autumn to late winter. In many areas, however, the climate is unpredictable and an early prune, say after a warm, wet spell towards the end of winter, can result in a rush of sappy growth that is damaged by an unexpected, late hard frost. The damage is seldom lasting, but growth will be checked and you will have to prune again to remove the frosted stems. Where

winters are harsh, therefore, delay pruning until early spring.

You can also prune late to delay flowering. If the rose is in a container you can prune as soon as the days begin to lengthen, bringing the plant under glass for early flowers (known as forcing). Commercial growers who exhibit at spring horticultural shows regularly force their plants in this way. Extra heat and light may also be necessary.

Tools

Secateurs (pruners) are suitable for most rose pruning, but you may need loppers (long-handled pruners) or a pruning saw to cut through the thick stems of older plants. Always use well-maintained tools with clean, sharp blades, as blunt tools will tear and snag the wood, providing an entry point for disease. After use, clean the blades with an oily rag.

■ RIGHT
Prune to create a balanced, open framework that allows good air circulation.

Making the cuts

Growth buds lie alternately on rose stems. Since the new growth will arise from the bud nearest the cut, prune to a bud that faces in the direction you want the new shoot to grow. Cut just above the bud, angling the cut away from the emerging growth. Cut out all dead, diseased or damaged wood. Also remove stems that cross, or are badly placed. On newly planted roses, cut back the remaining stems lightly to stimulate fresh growth. On established plants, cut back to ground level any old, woody, unproductive stems. If the rose is weak-growing, or if you want a few long stems for cutting, cut back the remaining stems by up to two-thirds. On vigorous roses, trim back lightly. A selective approach is often best, whereby you remove some stems, shorten others by a third or more, and leave the remainder unpruned or lightly trimmed.

Deadheading

Removing the flowers as they fade is essential if the roses are to reach their full potential, diverting energy from hip production towards further flowering. Systematically take off the fading flowers, cutting just above a bud facing in the desired direction of growth. After the first main flush, feed the roses well.

Renovation

Very old, neglected roses that have accumulated a quantity of unproductive wood can be given a new lease of life by hard pruning.

In late winter or early spring, cut the oldest, thickest stems back to ground level. Shorten the remainder to within 15–30cm (6–12in) of the ground. Feed the plant well, water and mulch. New growth will be vigorous, but it is likely to be a year or two before the flowering capacity is fully restored.

If the rose does not make good growth during the season following renovation, it is beyond salvation.

■ ABOVE
Removing faded blooms prolongs the display. Cut just above a growth bud.

Propagation

Commercially, roses are propagated by grafting material from named varieties on to vigorous seedling rootstocks. Rootstocks are not widely available outside the trade, so amateur gardeners usually choose one of the methods described here. In general, only the more vigorous varieties will root readily and make good plants.

Hardwood cuttings

Hardwood cuttings are taken around the end of the growing season, when top-growth has ceased and fully ripened. They can be rooted in the open ground provided there is some shelter from strong winds. Check the cuttings periodically during the winter. If a hard frost erodes the soil and causes the surface to crack open, firm in the cuttings. In very cold areas, protect them with a cloche. The cuttings should have rooted by the following autumn, and can be planted in their final positions the spring or autumn afterwards.

Semi-ripe cuttings

If winters are very severe, you may have more success with semi-ripe cuttings. These are taken from mid- to late summer when the

1 Prepare a trench about 23–30cm (9–12in) deep in the open ground, and line it to one-third of its depth with a layer of sharp sand.

3 Dip the base of the cutting in hormone rooting powder, and tap off the excess.

2 Cut well-ripened, pencil-thick stems from the rose. Remove the soft tip and trim to a length of about 23cm (9in), the base cut just below a leaf joint. Remove any leaves that remain on the stem.

4 Insert the cutting in the trench, leaving about 7.5cm (3in) above the soil surface. Firm the cuttings in.

growth is still green and pliable, but is beginning to turn woody at the base.

Prepare a rooting medium of equal parts peat (or a substitute) and sharp sand. Take a cutting just above an outward-facing bud. Trim the cutting at the base, just below a leaf joint, then cut back the soft tip to leave a stem length of about 10cm (4in). Remove the lower leaves and all the thorns, if any. Dip the base of the cutting in hormone rooting powder,

and insert it up to two-thirds of its length in 8cm (3in) or 13cm (5in) pots of the rooting medium. Firm the cuttings with your fingers, then spray with a fungicide both to moisten the compost and to kill any fungal spores and bacteria.

Label the cuttings, and tent the pot with a polythene (plastic) bag supported on canes or wire hoops. Keep in a shady, frost-free place. You should check the cuttings periodically

LAYERING

1 Select a pliable shoot that can be brought down to ground level from near the base of the plant. Cut off all the leaves and side shoots from a section about 30cm (1ft) long.

2 Around the point where the stem will meet the ground, work in peat or an alternative to make the soil more friable.

3 With a sharp knife, cut a tongue in the wood on the underside of the stem.

4 Keep the tongue open with a small piece of wood, or a matchstick, and dust the cut surfaces with hormone rooting powder.

5 Bring the stem down to the ground. To keep the wound just below soil level, fasten down the stem with a length of wire bent into a U shape.

6 Bend the shoot tip upwards and secure it to a cane inserted in the ground with lengths of wire or horticultural string tied in figures of eight.

and remove any fallen leaves, which may rot. Make sure that the rooting medium stays fairly moist, keeping it watered with a fungicidal solution. The cuttings should have rooted by the following spring. Plant them out in nursery beds or pot them up individually in loam-based compost (soil mix) (John Innes No. 3). Continue to grow on until they are large enough to plant in their final positions.

Layering

This is a good method for roses that have long, flexible stems that can be brought down to ground level. Ground-cover roses can often be increased by this technique since they are descendants of climbing species, and may even layer themselves in favourable conditions. It can be a more reliable technique than cuttings because the new plant remains

attached to the parent while rooting. However, it is usually feasible to produce only a few new plants by this method, since only a small number of stems is likely to be suitable.

Roses are best layered in late summer. The layers should have rooted by the following spring when they can be severed from the parent, and potted up or grown on in a nursery bed until large enough to plant out in their final positions.

Hybridization

This is the process by which new plant varieties are produced. It can occur in the wild, where two compatible species grow in close proximity to one another, but the vast majority of garden hybrids arise as a result of deliberate crossing.

Hybridization is a sexual method of producing new plants. In common with the majority of flowering plants, roses have flowers with both male and female reproductive parts. To produce fertile seed, pollen, borne on the stamens (male) from one flower, is brought into contact with the stigmas (female) of another. Seed develops in the ovary below the stigmas. Seedlings will share some characteristics with both parents without being identical to either.

Rose breeders practise the method of hybridization extensively. In any one year, hundreds of crosses are made, but only a few of the resulting plants have commercial potential. To be commercially viable, a new rose must be vigorous, hardy and disease-resistant, with good colour and scent, and of sufficient novelty to distinguish it from existing roses. One or more of these attributes may be absent if the rose scores highly in other categories. All new roses have to undergo extensive trials before large-scale

1 Select the seed parent. Choose a flower that is not fully open and is unlikely to have been pollinated. Working from the outside, carefully pull off the petals.

2 Carefully remove the stamens with sterilized tweezers.

6 When fully open, pull away all the petals to expose the reproductive parts of the plant.

7 Uncover the seed parent, and brush the anthers of the pollen parent across the stigmas of the seed parent to transfer the pollen. Replace the bag and allow the hip to develop. Label the stem with the names of both parents.

production can be considered. Given the fierce competition, it is unlikely that the amateur will raise a new rose with any significant future, but you can still produce good garden plants.

Since the rose as a genus has a vast gene pool and extensive interbreeding has already occurred, you can never be certain which characteristics will arise from any cross. Seedlings may bear no visible resemblance to either of their parents. The pedigrees of many

modern roses are given in *Modern Roses*, published by the American Rose Society, but beyond a certain point the ancestry of all rose hybrids is conjectural.

Theoretically, all roses should cross with each other, but some varieties are so highly bred that they are sterile (mules), or partly so. Also, some varieties make better pollen parents than seed parents, and vice versa; in any breeding programme it

3 When you have removed the stamens, you should be left with the bare stigmas.

4 To prevent pollination from another source, cover the flower with a paper or plastic bag secured with a wire tie.

5 Cut a flower that is not fully open from the pollen parent, and keep it in water indoors.

8 Once the hip is ripe, cut it from the plant and slice it open to extract the seed. Mix the extracted seed with peat, or an alternative, and grit or perlite in a plastic bag. Place it in a refrigerator for three or four weeks.

9 Sow the seed in trays or pots of seed compost (growing medium), and cover with grit.

10 Label the pots and place them in a cold frame to overwinter.

is worth making the cross in both directions. When recording crosses, the convention is to cite the seed parent first, so, for example, label the seedlings 'Blue Moon' × 'Allgold', or 'Allgold' × 'Blue Moon', depending on which way you made the cross.

Rose seedlings can flower in their first year, though the blooms may not be typical. It will be a few years before you know whether you have produced an outstanding newcomer.

GENETIC ENGINEERING

The technique of genetic engineering is a sometimes controversial method whereby specific genes (often from a different genus) are introduced into cells to ensure that a particular characteristic is inherited. Hitherto, its use has been largely confined to commercial, edible crop production, usually to promote disease-resistance or a long shelf-life in food crops.

There is every reason to suppose that in time the techniques will be applied to ornamental plants, creating roses that are particularly disease-resistant or hold their petals for a longer period, for instance. It should also be possible to extend the colour range to include the elusive blue. Genetic engineering requires laboratory conditions, and is beyond the reach of the amateur gardener.

Roses as cut flowers

Roses are the archetypal flower arranger's flower. They are beautiful at all stages, whether as tightly scrolled buds or at the height of their elegance just before they are fully open, becoming voluptuous as they age. The colour range is probably unmatched by any other flower, whether you are looking for delicate pastels or strong, vibrant reds, yellows and oranges. They last well in both water and florist's foam, besides being the traditional choice for buttonholes.

Gather flowers for arranging as early in the day as possible, when plant tissues are at their most turgid after the night dew. To increase your options when arranging, cut them with as long a stem as possible, cutting just above a leaf joint. For the longest-lived arrangements, they should be still in bud but with the sepals fully reflexed. Immediately on cutting, stand the stems in deep water until you are ready to arrange them.

If you are arranging in water, begin by removing from the lower part of the stem all the leaves that would otherwise be below water.

ROSES FOR ARRANGING

Most varieties provide good cut flowers, the following being among the most long-lasting:

'Alec's Red' (red)

'Alexander' (red)

'Allgold' (yellow)

'Anne Harkness' (apricot-yellow)

'Arthur Bell' (yellow)

'Big Purple' (purplish-red)

'Blue Moon' (lilac-pink)

'City of London' (pale pink)

'Double Delight' (cream, edged warm pink)

'Dutch Gold' (yellow)

'Elina' (ivory-white)

'Elizabeth Harkness' (white)

'Escapade' (pink)

'Fragrant Cloud' (scarlet)

'Grandpa Dickson' (primrose yellow)

'Hannah Gordon' (white, edged pink)

'Iceberg' (white)

'Ingrid Bergman' (red)

'Julia's Rose' (brownish-pink)

'Just Joey' (orange)

'King's Ransom' (yellow)

'Margaret Merril' (white)

'My Choice' (salmon-pink)

'Papa Meilland' (red)

'Pascali' (white)

'Paul Shirville' (pink)

'Peace' (yellow and pink)

'Polar Star' (creamy-white)

'Precious Platinum' (red)

'Princess Michael of Kent' (yellow)

'Queen Elizabeth' (pink)

'Red Devil' (red)

'Rosemary Harkness' (orange)

'Royal Highness' (pale pink)

'Royal William' (red)

'Savoy Hotel' (light pink)

'Sexy Rexy' (light rose-pink)

'Sheila's Perfume' (yellow, edged red)

'Whisky Mac' (orange)

■ BELOW

Cut roses for arranging with as long a stem as possible.

If left, they may rot, shortening the life of the arrangement and creating an unpleasant smell. Trim the base of the stems with a slanting cut. This facilitates water uptake, and makes the stems easier to insert in florist's foam. If you wish, you can remove any thorns, either by scraping down the stems with a knife or, if the stems are ripe, by snapping them off between finger and thumb.

Prolong the life of arrangements in water by adding proprietary cut-flower food. While arrangements in florist's foam often have greater visual impact, they are usually shorter-lived since you cannot feed the flowers after arranging. You can, however, keep the arrangement fresh by periodically spraying with distilled water at room temperature.

If you buy roses from a florist, prepare the stems as described, then stand them in a bucket of deep water for at least one hour before arranging.

DISBUDDING

Sometimes practised by exhibitors and flower arrangers, this is a means of producing prime-quality blooms on large-flowered roses. It also ensures that all the flowers in a cluster open simultaneously on cluster-flowered roses.

Roses can be disbudded in mid- to late spring as the flower buds are swelling, before they begin to show colour, as well as later in the season when any new buds are at a similar stage. On large-flowered roses, pinch out between finger and thumb any small buds that develop in the leaf axils below the main bud at the end of the stem. On cluster-flowered roses, pinch out the central bud of the truss.

■ LEFT

Disbudding large-flowered roses ensures prime-quality blooms for arranging.

■ LEFT

A fresh and contemporary flower arrangement using florist's foam to position the roses in galvanized buckets.

Pests, diseases and other disorders

Most roses are prone to certain pests and diseases, but fortunately most are easy to control. The incidence of disease and pest attack is, to some extent, due to the climate and regional variations. For example, blackspot is more prevalent in some parts of the country than in others, while mildew is more likely to occur in dry weather, and greenfly (aphid) populations are partly regulated by the winter survival of their predators.

Some rose varieties are more susceptible to problems than others, but well-fed roses that are growing strongly usually shake off the effects of any attack, provided you act quickly. Maintaining good standards of garden hygiene decreases the likelihood and the severity of any problems: you should regularly clear up any plant debris, such as fallen leaves, that may rot and harbour disease from the roses as well as other plants. Also burn, or otherwise dispose of, any rose prunings for the same reason; do not compost them.

Systemic insecticides and fungicides are applied as a spray and are absorbed by the plant. They do not kill the pest or disease directly, so their effect is not immediate. Repeated applications are usually necessary. The following are some of the problems you are most likely to encounter in the garden.

Aphids

How to identify: Roses are most likely to be attacked by greenfly. They are usually spotted near the start of the season on the ends of stems and developing flowerbuds.
Cause: Failure to destroy prunings from the previous season that may harbour eggs, though in practice this pest is virtually endemic and you are likely to encounter it every season.
Control: Spray the plants with a proprietary systemic insecticide as soon as you notice an infestation, and repeat as directed by the manufacturer. Some insecticides are selective in their action and leave beneficial insects, such as ladybirds, unharmed. Organic alternatives include soft soap and insecticides based on derris or pyrethrum.

Aphids

Although infestations may be heavy, the pest is easy to control and long-term damage can be avoided.

Balling

How to identify: Petals turn brown and cling together so that the flowers fail to open.
Cause: Prolonged wet weather while the buds are developing. Greenfly infestations earlier in the season can also lead to balling.

Balling

Control: Not possible. Balling is a seasonal problem that does not affect the health of the plant overall, but you should remove balled flowers that may otherwise rot and allow diseases to strike.

Blackspot

How to identify: Black spots or patches develop on the leaves and, in some cases, the stems, from mid-summer onwards. The leaves yellow and eventually drop. Untreated plants die back.

Blackspot

Cause: A bacterium that overwinters in the soil and enters the plant during the growing season. Leaving infected prunings on the ground increases the likelihood of an attack.
Control: Remove all infected leaves and stems and destroy them, then spray the plant with Bordeaux mixture. If you need to cut the plant hard back, feed and water well to encourage recovery. Blackspot is more common in certain geographical areas, and certain rose varieties are more susceptible than others. In severe cases, replace with disease-resistant and guaranteed disease-free stock.

Powdery mildew

How to identify: A whitish-grey powdering on the leaves and stems which, if left untreated, can cover the whole plant.
Cause: Various fungi that thrive in dry soil. They are most likely to cause damage where the air is stagnant.

Mildew

Control: Spray with a proprietary fungicide. Thin out congested growth. Where the overall planting is thick, and air circulation is poor, replant to ensure more space around the plants.

Rust

How to identify: Orange spots that then turn black appear on the undersides of leaves from mid-summer onwards. If left untreated, rose rusts can be fatal.
Cause: Fungal spores that are more prevalent in humid weather.
Control: Remove infected parts then spray with a fungicide. Improve air circulation around the plants, as for mildew.

Rust

Suckering

How to identify: Strong shoots arise from the rootstock, often at some distance from the plant. They also occur on the main stems of standards. Left in place they will rob the rose of nutrients.
Cause: Damage to the root system, usually through digging around the base of the plant. Modern rootstocks have a lesser tendency to sucker, but suckers are always likely to occur on standards, since the rootstock is above ground level.

Suckering

Control: Scrape away the soil around the sucker until you find its point of origin. Pull it sharply away from the roots. On standards, rub out emerging buds on the main stem or, if they are long shoots, cut them back to their point of origin.

Dieback

How to identify: Flowerbuds fail to mature and wither. Beginning at the tip of the

Dieback

stem, leaves begin to wither and drop. The stem droops and may blacken.
Cause: Any of the above diseases, uncontrolled, can lead to dieback. The condition can also be caused by other fungi or bacteria, frost damage, or a lack of soil nutrients, particularly potassium and phosphorus.
Control: Cut back all affected growth to clean, healthy wood, then feed the plant well. If dieback occurs in the autumn, do not feed until the following spring, since any new growth will be susceptible to winter frost damage.

Proliferation

How to identify: The stem continues to grow through the open flower, producing a further bud or cluster of buds.
Cause: Damage to the stem while it is growing, either by frost or a virus.
Control: Cut off affected stems. If only one or a few stems are affected, further steps are unnecessary, but

Proliferation

where the whole plant has the condition a virus is probably the culprit, and the whole plant should be dug up and destroyed.

Rose-sick soil

How to identify: The roses suddenly fail to thrive and die back.
Cause: Complex, and associated with nutrient exhaustion in the soil since it often occurs in ground that has supported roses for a number of years.
Control: Dig up and discard any affected roses before replacing the topsoil, i.e. the top 60cm (2ft) of soil. Replant with fresh stock.

Effects of rose-sick soil

Calendar

■ LEFT
Plant early-flowering and late-flowering rose varieties in the same bed to extend the season for colourful displays from early summer right through to late autumn.

Early spring

Improve the soil and plant new stock. On established plants, cut out any dead, diseased or damaged wood, and shorten the remaining stems. Fork rose fertilizer around the base as new growth emerges, water in well, and mulch. Renovate any old or neglected plants.

Mid- to late spring

Check for, and begin control of, aphid infestations. Remove any suckers. Plant new stock.

Pre-empt trouble by spraying against greenfly in spring.

Mid-summer

Deadhead and boost with rose fertilizer. Trim hedges lightly, then feed. Increase your stock by taking semi-ripe cuttings, by layering or budding. Check for, and control, blackspot, rust and mildew. Continue to keep a watch for suckers. Plant new stock (container-grown only).

Late summer

Continue to take semi-ripe cuttings of vigorous plants, or layer them, if suitable.

You can disbud roses throughout the summer months.

Autumn

Fork in bonemeal around the base of the plants, water in well, and mulch. Plant new stock. Take hardwood cuttings of vigorous roses.

Late winter

Tidy up hedges, if necessary. In exposed sites, shorten the stems of specimens to prevent wind-rock. In frosty weather, where the ground cracks and opens up, firm in hardwood cuttings.

Other recommended modern roses

In addition to the roses illustrated in the Directory, the following are also recommended. Synonyms and the date of introduction follow the name of the rose in parentheses. The dimensions given are what will be achieved with good cultivation, the first figure indicating the rose's final height, the second its spread.

'Abbeyfield Rose' (syn. 'Cocbrose'; 1985) Large-flowered rose with fully double, lightly scented, deep pink flowers from summer to autumn. 75cm (2½ft) x 60cm (2ft). Good for bedding.
'Agnes' (1992) Rugosa rose with double, scented, pale yellow flowers in summer. 2m (6ft) x 1.2m (4ft). Healthy and versatile .
'Allgold' (1956) Cluster-flowered rose with double, scented, bright yellow flowers throughout summer and autumn. 75cm (2½ft) x 50cm (20in). A good bedding rose.
'Alpine Sunset' (1974) Large-flowered rose with fully double, fragrant, warm apricot-pink flowers from summer to autumn. 60cm (2ft) x 60cm (2ft). Best with protection from cold weather.
'Anisley Dickson' (syn. 'Dickimono', 'Dicky'; 1983) Cluster-flowered rose with double, only lightly scented,

salmon-pink flowers from summer to autumn. 90cm (3ft) x 75cm (2½ft). Good in containers.
'Anna Livia' (syn. 'Kormeter', 'Trier 2000'; 1985) Cluster-flowered rose with double, fragrant, clear pink flowers from summer to autumn. 75cm (2½ft) x 60cm (2ft). Makes a good low hedge.

'Blessings'

'Blessings' (1968) Large-flowered rose with fully double, lightly scented, warm pink flowers from summer to autumn. 90cm (3ft) x 75cm (2½ft). Disease-resistant.
'Bright Smile' (syn. 'Dicdance'; 1980) Cluster-flowered rose with semi-double, fragrant, clear yellow flowers that open flat from summer to autumn. 45cm (1½ft) x 45cm (1½ft). Rain-resistant.
'Broadlands' (syn. 'Sonnenschirm', 'Tanmirsch';

1993) Ground-cover rose with double, fragrant, soft creamy yellow flowers from summer to autumn. 75cm (2½ft) x 1.2m (4ft). Suitable for containers.
'Carefree Beauty' (1977) Ground-cover rose with semi-double, fragrant, creamy buff-pink flowers throughout summer. 1.2m (5ft) x 1.2m (4ft). Spreading.
'Champagne Cocktail' (syn. 'Horflash'; 1985) Cluster-flowered rose with double, fragrant, yellow flowers suffused pink from summer to autumn. 90cm (3ft) x 60cm (2ft). Good for bedding.
'Chanelle' (1959) Cluster-flowered rose with semi-double to double, fragrant, creamy buff-pink flowers through summer and autumn. 75cm (2½ft) x 60cm (2ft). Good disease resistance.
'Chatsworth' (syn. 'Mirato', 'Tanotari', 'Tanotax'; 1990) Ground-cover rose with double, fragrant, rich pink flowers from summer to autumn. 60cm (2ft) x 90cm (3ft). A good short standard.
'Cider Cup' (syn. 'Dicladida'; 1988) Dwarf cluster-flowered rose with double, virtually scentless, apricot-orange flowers from summer to autumn. 45cm (1½ft) x 90cm (3ft). A very good short standard.

'City of Leeds' (1966) Cluster-flowered rose with lightly scented, salmon-pink flowers from summer to autumn. 75cm (2½ft) x 60cm (2ft). Good for bedding.
'City of London' (syn. 'Harukfore'; 1988) Cluster-flowered rose with double, fragrant, soft pink flowers from summer to autumn. 2m (6ft) x 1.2m (4ft). Use for bedding or as a specimen.
'Congratulations' (syn. 'Korlift', 'Sylvia'; 1978) Large-flowered rose with fully double, fragrant, deep pink flowers from summer to autumn. 1.2m (4ft) x 90cm (3ft). Can grow taller with good conditions.

'Dawn Chorus'

'Conservation' (syn. 'Cocdimple'; 1988) Dwarf cluster-flowered rose with semi-double, fragrant, apricot-orange flowers fading to pink from summer to autumn. 45cm (1½ft) x 45cm (1½ft). Good for bedding.

'Crimson Glory' (1935) Large-flowered rose with fully double, strongly fragrant, deep red flowers in summer and autumn. 60cm (2ft) x 60cm (2ft). Good for cutting.

'Dawn Chorus' (syn. 'Dicquasar'; 1993) Large-flowered rose with double, only lightly scented, orange flowers with yellow petal reverses from summer to autumn. 75cm (2½ft) x 60cm (2ft). Good in containers.

'Dearest' (1960) Cluster-flowered rose with double, fragrant, clear pink flowers from summer to autumn. 60cm (2ft) x 60cm (2ft). A good bedding rose.

'Deep Secret' (1977) Large-flowered rose with double, fragrant, deep red flowers from summer to autumn. 90cm (3ft) x 75cm (2½ft). Good for cutting.

'Disco Dancer' (syn. 'Dicinfra'; 1984) Cluster-flowered rose with semi-double, only lightly scented, bright orange-red flowers from summer to autumn. 75cm (2½ft) x 60cm (2ft). Good in a container.

'Doris Tysterman' (1975) Large-flowered rose with fully double, fragrant, coppery orange flowers from summer to autumn. 1.2m (4ft) x 75cm (2½ft). Good for bedding.

'Deep Secret'

'Drummer Boy' (syn. 'Harvacity'; 1987) Dwarf cluster-flowered rose with semi-double, only lightly scented, brilliant crimson flowers from summer to autumn. 50cm (20in) x 50cm (20in). Profuse.

'Ena Harkness' (1946) Large-flowered rose with fully double, fragrant, deep red flowers from early summer to autumn. 75cm (2½ft) x 60cm (2ft). Needs good cultivation.

'English Miss' (1978) Cluster-flowered rose with fully double, camellia-like, fragrant, soft pink flowers from summer to autumn. 75cm (2½ft) x 60cm (2ft). Good in containers.

'Ernest H. Morse' (1965) Large-flowered rose with double, fragrant, red flowers that age darker from summer to autumn. 75cm (2½ft) x 60cm (2ft). Free-flowering.

'Evelyn Fison' (syn. 'Irish Wonder', 'Macev'; 1962) Cluster-flowered rose with double, virtually scentless, brilliant red flowers from summer to autumn. 70cm (28in) x 60cm (2ft). Good for bedding.

'Fellowship' (syn. 'Harwelcome', 'Livin' Easy'; 1992) Cluster-flowered rose with double, fragrant, warm orange flowers from summer to autumn. 75cm (2½ft) x 60cm (2ft). Good for bedding.

'Ferdy' (syn. 'Ferdi', 'Keitoly'; 1984) Ground-cover rose with dense clusters of small, double, only lightly scented, bright pink flowers. 80cm (32in) x 1.2m (4ft). Irregular habit.

'Festival' (syn. 'Kordialo'; 1994) Dwarf cluster-flowered rose with fully double, only lightly scented, rich scarlet flowers from summer to autumn. 60cm (2ft) x 50cm (20in). A good standard.

'Fragrant Delight' (1978) Cluster-flowered rose with double, fragrant, salmon-orange flowers from summer to autumn. 90cm (3ft) x 75cm (2½ft). Needs good cultivation.

'Frau Dagmar Hastrup' (syn. 'Frau Dagmar Hartopp'; 1914) Rugosa rose with single, fragrant, pale pink flowers with golden stamens

in summer followed by tomato-red hips. 90cm (3ft) x 1.2m (4ft). Excellent as a low hedge.

'Fred Loads' (1967) Cluster-flowered rose with semi-double, scented, soft orange-vermilion flowers from summer to autumn. 2m (6½ft) x 90cm (3ft). Good as a hedge or specimen.

'Freedom' (syn. 'Dicjem'; 1984) Large-flowered rose with double, only lightly scented, vivid yellow flowers from summer to autumn. 75cm (2½ft) x 60cm (2ft). Good for bedding.

'Doris Tysterman'

'Gentle Touch' (syn. 'Diclulu'; 1986) Dwarf cluster-flowered rose with double, slightly fragrant, pale salmon-pink flowers from summer to autumn. 40cm (16in) x 40cm (16in). Suitable for containers and ground cover.

'Glenfiddich' (1976) Cluster-flowered rose with double, fragrant, golden-yellow flowers from summer to autumn. 75cm (2½ft) x 60cm (2ft). Needs good cultivation.

'Grouse' (syn. 'Immensee', 'Korimo', 'Lac Rose'; 1984) Ground-cover rose with single, fragrant, pale pink flowers that open flat to reveal golden stamens from mid- to late summer. 1.2m (4ft) x 3m (10ft). Good in a wild garden.

'Hakuun' (1962) Dwarf cluster-flowered rose with semi-double, fragrant, light buff-yellow flowers from summer to autumn. 40cm (16in) x 45cm (1½ft). Prolific.

'Harvest Fayre' (syn. 'Dicnorth'; 1990) Cluster-flowered rose with double, fragrant, apricot-yellow flowers from summer to late autumn. 75cm (2½ft) x 60cm (2ft). Deadhead to prolong flowering.

'Hertfordshire' (syn. 'Kortenay', 'Tommeliese'; 1991) Ground-cover rose with single, fragrant, vivid pink flowers from summer to autumn. 45cm (1½ft) x 90cm (3ft). Best with minimum pruning.

'Hula Girl' (1975) Miniature rose with fully double, fragrant, salmon-orange flowers from summer to autumn. 45cm (1½ft) x 40cm

(16in). Good for bedding.

'Iced Ginger' (1971) Cluster-flowered rose with double, only lightly scented, coppery pink flowers from summer to autumn. 90cm (3ft) x 70cm (28in). Good in flower arrangements.

'Josephine Bruce' (1952) Large-flowered rose with shapely, double, very fragrant, rich deep crimson-red flowers. 75cm (2½ft) x 60cm (2ft). A good standard.

'Keepsake' (syn. 'Esmeralda', 'Kormalda'; 1980) Large-flowered rose with fully double, fragrant, warm pink flowers from summer to autumn. 75cm (2½ft) x 60cm (2ft). Rain-resistant.

'Lovely Lady'

'Kent' (syn. 'Poulcov', 'Pyrenees', 'Sparkler', 'White Cover'; 1988) Ground-cover rose with semi-double, virtually scentless, white flowers from summer to

autumn. 55cm (22in) x 90cm (3ft). An effective standard.

'Little Bo-Peep' (syn. 'Poullen'; 1992) Dwarf cluster-flowered rose with semi-double, virtually scentless, pale pink flowers from summer to autumn. 30cm (1ft) x 50cm (20in). Prolific.

'Lovely Lady' (syn. 'Dicjubell', 'Dickson's Jubilee'; 1986) Large-flowered rose with fully double, fragrant, warm pink flowers from summer to autumn. 80cm (32in) x 70cm (28in). Needs good cultivation.

'Lovers' Meeting' (1980) Large-flowered rose with double, fragrant, warm pinkish-orange flowers from summer to autumn. 75cm (2½ft) x 75cm (2½ft). Makes a good standard.

'Matangi' (syn. 'Macman'; 1974) Cluster-flowered rose with double, only lightly scented, brilliant vermilion flowers with white eyes and petal edges. 80cm (32in) x 60cm (2ft). Best with good cultivation.

'Max Graf' (1919) Ground-cover or rugosa rose with single, fragrant, deep pink flowers with golden stamens during summer. 60cm (2ft) x 2.4m (8ft). Good in a wild garden.

'Melody Maker' (syn. 'Dicqueen'; 1991)

Cluster-flowered rose with double, only lightly scented, vivid vermilion-red flowers from summer to autumn. 70cm (28in) x 60cm (2ft). Makes a good standard.

'Oranges and Lemons'

'Mischief' (syn. 'Macmi'; 1961) Large-flowered rose with double, only lightly scented, deep salmon-pink flowers from summer to autumn. 1m (3ft) x 60cm (2ft). Rust may be a problem.

'Nathalie Nypels' (1919) Cluster-flowered or polyantha rose with semi-double, sweetly scented, rose-pink flowers, fading to blush-pink, from summer to autumn. 60cm (2ft) x 60cm (2ft). Deadhead regularly to maintain flowering.

'National Trust' (syn. 'Bad Nauheim'; 1970) Large-flowered rose with fully double, virtually scentless, vivid red flowers from summer to autumn. 60cm (2ft) x 60cm (2ft). Free-flowering.

'Simba'

'News' (syn. 'Legnews'; 1968) Cluster-flowered rose with double, only lightly scented, deep red flowers that open flat from summer to autumn. 60cm (2ft) x 50cm (20in). Rain-resistant.

'Northamptonshire' (syn. 'Mattdor'; 1988) Ground-cover rose with semi-double, fragrant, pale pink flowers from summer to autumn. 45cm (1½ft) x 90cm (3ft). Best in full sun.

'Nozomi' (1968) Ground-cover rose with single, only lightly scented, very pale pink to white flowers in mid-summer. 45cm (1½ft) x 1.5m (5ft). Stems will root where they touch the ground.

'Orange Sunblaze' (syn. 'Meijikitar', 'Orange Meillandina', 'Sunblaze';

1981) Miniature rose with fully double, only lightly scented, bright vermilion-orange flowers. 30cm (1ft) x 30cm (1ft). Excellent where space is limited.

'Oranges and Lemons' (syn. 'Macoranlem'; 1993) Cluster-flowered rose with double, fragrant, yellow flowers striped and splashed scarlet, from summer to autumn. 80cm (32in) x 60cm (2ft). Good for bedding.

'Piccolo' (syn. 'Piccola', 'Tanolokip'; 1984) Cluster-flowered rose with double, virtually scentless, vivid red flowers from summer to autumn. 50cm (20in) x 50cm (20in). Rain-resistant.

'Pink Bells' (syn. 'Poulbells'; 1983) Ground-cover rose with fully double, virtually scentless, clear pink flowers in mid-summer. 75cm (2½ft) x 1.5m (5ft). Free-flowering.

'Pink Grootendorst' (1923) Rugosa rose with double, scentless, clear pink flowers with frilled petals. 2m (6½ft) x 1.5m (5ft).

'Pot o' Gold' (syn. 'Dicdivine'; 1980) Large-flowered rose, fully double, fragrant, golden-yellow flowers from summer to autumn. 75cm (2½ft) x 60cm (2ft). Makes a good standard.

'Precious Platinum' (1974) Large-flowered rose with fully double, only lightly scented,

luminous red flowers. 90cm (3ft) x 60cm (2ft). Suitable for forcing under glass.

'Pretty Polly' (syn. 'Meitonje', 'Pink Symphony', 'Sweet Sunblaze'; 1989) Dwarf cluster-flowered rose with double, only lightly scented, rose-pink flowers from summer to autumn. 40cm (16in) x 45cm (1½ft). Prolific.

'Prima Ballerina' (syn. 'Première Ballerine'; 1957) Large-flowered rose with double, sweetly scented, warm pink flowers from summer to autumn. 90cm (3ft) x 60cm (2ft). Good for hedging.

'Tequila Sunrise'

'Princess Michael of Kent' (syn. 'Harlightly'; 1981) Cluster-flowered rose with fully double, sweetly scented, clear yellow flowers from summer to autumn. 60cm (2ft) x 50cm (20in). Good in containers.

'Red Ace' (syn. 'Amanda', 'Amruda'; 1982) Miniature rose with semi-double, virtually scentless, rich red flowers from summer to autumn. 30cm (1ft) x 30cm (1ft). Suitable for window boxes.

'Red Meidiland' (syn. 'Meineble', 'Rouge Meillandécar'; 1989) Ground-cover rose with single, only lightly scented, vivid red flowers from summer to autumn followed by orange-red hips. 75cm (2½ft) x 1.5m (5ft). Dead-head to ensure good fruiting.

'Remember Me' (syn. 'Cocdestin'; 1984) Large-flowered rose with fully double, only lightly scented, warm coppery orange flowers from summer to autumn. Best in a sheltered spot.

'Rose Gaujard' (syn. 'Gaumo'; 1957) Large-flowered rose with fully double, fragrant, cherry-red flowers that have pale pink petal reverses from summer to autumn. 90cm (3ft) x 75cm (2½ft). Beautiful in flower arrangements.

'Rosemary Harkness' (syn. 'Harrowbond'; 1985) Large-flowered rose with double, fragrant, orange-yellow to salmon-pink flowers from summer to autumn. 80cm (32in) x 80cm (32in). Weather-resistant.

'**Royal Highness**' (syn. 'Königliche Hoheit'; 1962) Large-flowered rose with shapely, fully double, strongly fragrant, flesh-pink flowers from summer to autumn. 90cm (3ft) or more x 60cm (2ft). Fares poorly in wet weather.

'**Sarah Van Fleet**' (1926) Rugosa rose with sweetly scented, light pink flowers that open to reveal yellow stamens from summer to autumn. 2m (6½ft) or more x 1.2m (4ft) or more. Makes an outstanding hedge.

'**Silver Jubilee**' (1978) Large-flowered rose with fully double, fragrant, soft pink flowers shaded with apricot-pink from summer to autumn. 90cm (3ft) x 75cm (2½ft). Free-flowering.

'**Simba**' (syn. 'Goldsmith', 'Helmut Schmidt', 'Korbelma'; 1981) Large-flowered rose with double, fragrant, clear yellow flowers from summer to autumn. 75cm (2½ft) x 60cm (2ft). Rain-resistant.

'**Snow Carpet**' (syn. 'Maccarpe'; 1980) Miniature or ground-cover rose with fully double, virtually scentless, creamy white flowers in mid-summer. 15cm (6in) x 50cm (20in). Makes a good short standard.

'**Starina**' (syn. 'Meigabi'; 1965) Miniature rose with double, scentless, vivid vermilion-orange flowers. 45cm (1½ft) x 35cm (14in). Vigorous and prolific.

'**Suma**' (syn. 'Harsuma'; 1989) Ground-cover rose with fully double, virtually scentless, deep pink flowers, sometimes margined white, from summer to autumn. 60cm (2ft) x 1.5m (5ft). Can be trained as a short climber.

'The Lady'

'**Surrey**' (syn. 'Korlanum', 'Sommerwind', 'Vent d'Eté'; 1985) Ground-cover rose with double, fragrant, salmon-pink flowers from summer to autumn. 80cm (32in) x 1.2m (4ft). Effective as a standard.

'**Sweet Magic**' (syn. 'Dicmagic'; 1987) Dwarf cluster-flowered rose with double, fragrant, warm yellow-orange flowers from summer to autumn. 40cm (16in) x 40cm (16in). Prolific.

'**Tango**' (syn. 'Macfirwal', 'Rock 'n' Roll', 'Stretch Johnson'; 1988) Cluster-flowered rose with semi-double, only lightly scented flowers; the petals, frilled at the edges, are orange-red with white rims, yellow at the base and on the reverse. 75cm (2½ft) x 60cm (2ft). Good for bedding.

'**Tequila Sunrise**' (syn. 'Beaulieu', 'Dicobey'; 1989) Large-flowered rose with double, only lightly scented, vivid yellow flowers with scarlet petal edges from summer to autumn. 75cm (2½ft) x 60cm (2ft). Dead-head to prolong flowering.

'**The Lady**' (syn. 'Fryjingo'; 1985) Large-flowered rose with double, fragrant, yellow flowers flushed salmon-pink from summer to autumn. 1m (3ft) x 60cm (2ft). Rain-resistant.

'**Top Marks**' (syn. 'Fryministar'; 1992) Dwarf cluster-flowered rose with fully double, virtually scentless, vivid orange-red flowers from summer to autumn. 45cm (1½ft) x 45cm (1½ft). Blackspot can sometimes be a problem.

'**Trumpeter**' (syn. 'Mactru'; 1977) Cluster-flowered rose with fully double, virtually scentless, rich red flowers from summer to autumn. 60cm (2ft) x 50cm (20in). Good as a standard.

'**Valencia**' (syn. 'Koreklia'; 1989) Large-flowered rose with double, fragrant, warm golden-yellow flowers from summer to autumn. 90cm (3ft) x 60cm (2ft). Can be taller; tolerates light shade.

'**Warm Wishes**' (syn. 'Fryxotic'; 1994) Large-flowered rose with double, fragrant, warm salmon-pink flowers from summer to autumn. 90cm (3ft) x 70cm (28in). Good for cutting.

'**Yvonne Rabier**' (1910) Miniature or polyantha rose with double, fragrant, creamy white flowers from summer to autumn. 45cm (1½ft) x 40cm (16in). Needs good cultivation.

'Warm Wishes'

Index

ACKNOWLEDGEMENTS
The author and publisher would
like to thank the following for
their help in making this book:
Anne Hartley, Long Buckby,
Northants; Gandy's Roses, North
Kilworth, Leics; Haddonstone
Ltd, East Haddon, Northants;
Mr and Mrs Smith, Nobottle,
Northants; RHS Wisley; Shirley
Allen, Long Buckby, Northants.
Thanks to Michelle Garrett for
the photograph on p55b.